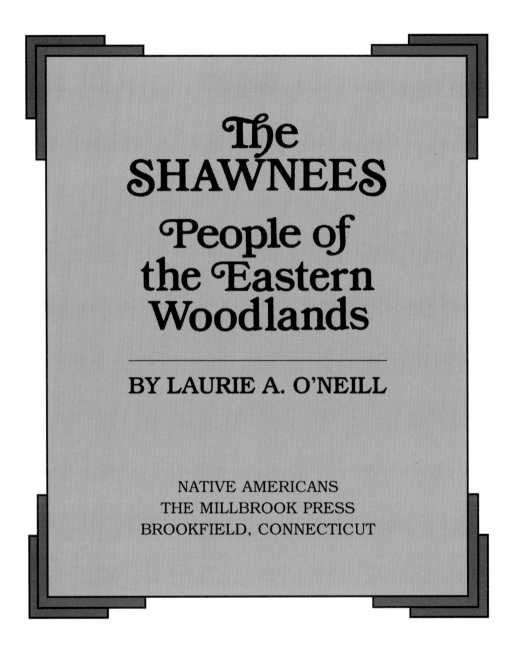

The SHAWNEES

People of the Eastern Woodlands

BY LAURIE A. O'NEILL

NATIVE AMERICANS
THE MILLBROOK PRESS
BROOKFIELD, CONNECTICUT

Cover: *Chicken Dance* by Earnest Spybuck, ca. 1910. Photo courtesy of the National Museum of the American Indian, Smithsonian Institution, catalog no. 2/6937 .

Photographs courtesy of North Wind Picture Archives: pp. 11, 14, 33, 43, 44, 47; National Archives Canada, Ottawa: p. 12 (*Battle of the Thames* by William Emmons, neg. no. C-41031); Cincinnati Historical Society: pp. 18, 24; National Museum of the American Indian, Smithsonian Institution: pp. 19 (cat. no. 3/36139), 21 (cat. no. 2/6927), 29 (neg. no. 19708), 30 (both, neg. no. 19751, neg. no. 19718), p. 50 (cat. no. 2/5785); New York Public Library, Rare Book Room: pp. 26, 42; Ohio Historical Society: p. 36; Bettmann Archive: p. 48; The Eastern Shawnee Tribe: p. 52. Map by Joe LeMonnier.

Library of Congress Cataloging-in-Publication Data
O'Neill, Laurie, 1949–
The Shawnees : people of the Eastern Woodlands / by Laurie A. O'Neill.
p.   cm. — (Native Americans)
Includes bibliographical references (p.   ) and index.
Summary: The history and culture of the Shawnees, probably the first Native Americans to settle the Ohio Valley and Great Lakes region.
ISBN 1-56294-533-5 (lib. bdg.)
1. Shawnee Indians — History — Juvenile literature.   2. Shawnee Indians — Social life and customs — Juvenile literature.   [1. Shawnee Indians.   2. Indians of North America.]   I. Title.   II. Series.
E99.S35064   1995   977'145111.004973 — dc20   94-42234   CIP   AC

CONTENTS

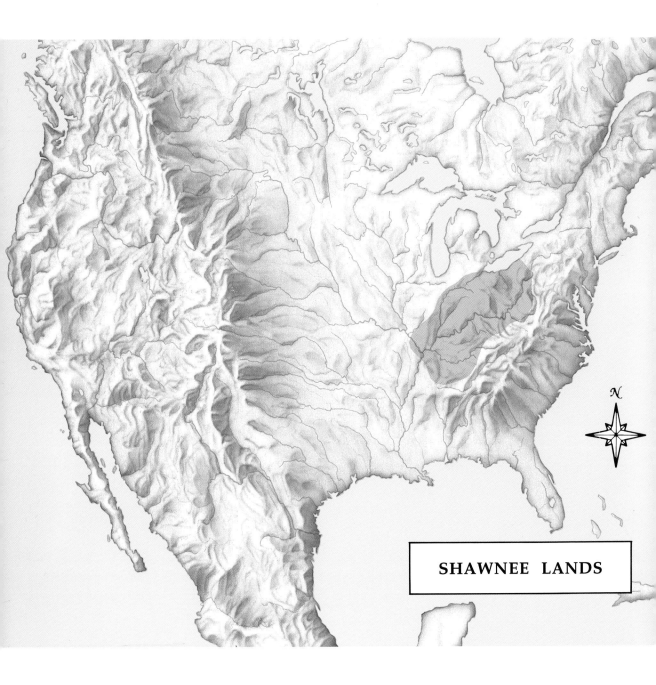

SHAWNEE LANDS

FACTS ABOUT
THE TRADITIONAL SHAWNEE
WAY OF LIFE

GROUP NAME:
Shawnee, from the Algonquian *sawanwa*,
"person of the south"

DIVISIONS:
Kispoko, Calaka, Thawikila, Mekoce, and Pekowi

GEOGRAPHICAL REGION:
Ohio River valley, Great Lakes area,
Cumberland River basin

LANGUAGE:
Shawnee (Algonquian family)

HOUSE TYPE:
Bark- or skin-covered lodge house

MAIN FOODS:
Corn, beans, squash, nuts, berries, and game

Chapter One

THE BATTLE OF THAMES

Although it was a mild October morning, Tecumseh felt a chill creep over him and he shuddered. The forty-five-year-old Shawnee chief gazed sadly at his trusted friends and advisers.

"Brother warriors," Tecumseh said. "We are now about to enter an engagement from which I shall never come out. My body," he told them, "will remain on the field of battle." Then he removed his elaborate headpiece, silver armlets, and other ornaments that distinguished him as a Shawnee chief.

Off, too, came the British dress coat, pistols, and gleaming sword once presented to him in friendship by a British general. These Tecumseh gave to his closest friends. The only weapon the Shawnee chief would carry into battle against the Americans that day was a war club given to him by his older brother.

Tecumseh now wore simple native dress: a fringed buckskin shirt, a pair of leggings, and a breechcloth. He tied a twisted red cloth around his head and added a white feather.

Soon the woods along the Thames River, just above Lake Erie in Ontario, Canada, were thick with soldiers. The Americans intended to drive the combined Indian and British forces out of this area near the Canadian border and make it a part of the United States.

Suddenly there was a burst of rifle fire and the thunder of horses' hooves. Over the next few hours a cloud of dust and smoke hung over the battlefield and cries of agony were heard as tomahawks, clubs, knives, and bullets found their marks.

Tecumseh, blood trickling down his face from a head wound, repeatedly plunged into the fray. He shouted words of encouragement to his warriors. *"Oui shi cat to oui!"* (pronounced "wee shee cah TOO wee") he cried. "Be strong!"

The British, however, had tired of the campaign early and they began to retreat, abandoning Tecumseh's forces. Despite being outnumbered, he and his warriors continued to fight.

Tearing off his bloodstained shirt, Tecumseh charged into a line of soldiers. He may have seen the rifle barrel leveled at his chest. But it did not matter. Within a moment one, then two, lead balls ripped through his heart and he fell to the ground, lifeless.

When Tecumseh's voice could no longer be heard over the din of battle, his warriors began to disappear into the forest. The chief had ordered them to retreat if he was killed.

Those who fought with Tecumseh that day represented many tribes. But it was the Shawnees who were especially devastated by the outcome. They had lost everything: the battle, their leader, and Tecumseh's dream, which they shared, of a united Indian nation.

*The great Shawnee leader Tecumseh, shown wearing
the formal clothing given to him by a British general.
The headdress is a turban decorated with an eagle feather;
around his neck hangs a King George III medal.*

*A lithograph by William Emmons shows
Tecumseh's death during the Battle of Thames.*

The Battle of Thames in 1813 marked the last Indian resistance against white settlement in the Great Lakes and Ohio Valley region, homeland of the Shawnees. It ended many years of bloody conflict and established white control over a vast area of Indian territory.

Although the Shawnees are one of the least-known Native American tribes, they played a major role in resisting white settlement in the Northeast. The struggle of the Shawnees and their legendary chief Tecumseh to save their ancestral lands is a compelling chapter in Native American history.

Chapter Two

WOODLAND WANDERERS

The word Shawnee is from the Algonquian *sawanwa*, which means "person of the south." The Shawnees were the southernmost of the Algonquian (al-GON-kee-in)-speaking peoples.

Long ago there were many language families in North America. At least thirty tribes belonged to the Algonquian group. They spoke different dialects or variations of the same language. Although the tribes shared a similar environment and had similar lifeways and traditions, not all of them got along, and some were bitter enemies.

The Shawnees were probably among the Algonquian tribes who migrated from the far northern region of Labrador on the eastern coast of Canada. They may have been the first Native Americans to inhabit the Ohio River valley and Great Lakes region, which became known as the Old Northwest.

From the 1600s through the early 1800s, the Shawnees lived mostly in Ohio, Kentucky, and in Tennessee's Cumberland River Basin. But they had hunting grounds and villages as

The lush vegetation along the banks of the Ohio River attracted the Shawnees as they moved into the Eastern Woodlands.

far south as West Virginia, South Carolina, and Georgia. There were also Shawnees in Illinois, Indiana, and Pennsylvania.

The Shawnees roamed throughout the area that was known as the Eastern Woodlands. This area covered the region from North Carolina to Canada, and from the Atlantic Coast to the Mississippi River. It was a vast wilderness of dark swamps, deep blue lakes, and dense forests crisscrossed by rivers and streams. The soil was rich and fertile, wildlife abounded, and the waters teemed with fish. Nuts, berries, and other wild edibles were plentiful. The forests provided wood and bark for building materials and fuel.

In small groups of extended families called bands, the Shawnees moved frequently through an area comprising fifteen present-day states. They migrated for many reasons. There was danger from more powerful enemy tribes such as the Iroquois, and the need for better farming or hunting land. Later, they were driven from their homes by white settlers and soldiers.

The Shawnees had great respect for the natural world, believing the Creator had put the animals and other resources there to help them survive. They had no formal boundaries or system of land ownership, but acknowledged each other's territory and often went to war against trespassers.

By the mid-1700s more than 3,000 Shawnees lived in dozens of villages along the Scioto (sy-OH-toe), Ohio, and Mad rivers in the Old Northwest. This area was considered the center of the Shawnee nation. At no other time in the tribe's history did such a large number of Shawnees live in one place.

Chapter Three

AN ANCIENT WAY OF LIFE

Shawnee society was very different from that of the white cultures the tribe would encounter. Such differences made it difficult for Native Americans and white people to understand one another.

DIVISIONS AND CLANS ▪ From earliest accounts the Shawnee tribe had five subdivisions, each with its own chiefs and responsibilities. The Kispoko (Tecumseh's people) planned and carried out warfare. The Calaka and the Thawikila divisions addressed political issues. The Mekoce were responsible for medicine and health, and the Pekowi took care of tribal ritual.

　　There were also many Shawnee clans, including Snake, Turtle, Turkey, Bear, Raccoon, Deer, Owl, Wolf, Lynx, Horse, Rabbit, and Loon. A clan was a group of families believed to be descended from the same male ancestor. The Shawnees believed the animal's spirit protected them.

GOVERNMENT ▪ The Shawnees governed themselves. They had no police, written laws, courts, or jails. Instead they followed a strict moral code in which honesty and loyalty were of utmost importance.

Tribal councils were made up of older Shawnees respected for their wisdom and experience who met to discuss important issues. Decisions were not usually made by one person, but were reached after long discussions were held until everyone agreed.

There was a system of punishment for misdeeds, such as stealing, hurting another person, lying, committing murder, and even gossiping. Wrongdoers might be flogged, exiled (sent away), or killed.

CHIEFS ▪ Shawnee chiefs could be men or women. Each band had one or more chiefs. A peace chief was the group's spiritual leader, and a war chief planned and led attacks on the enemy. Female chiefs might direct certain tribal ceremonies and rituals, or help keep peace within their villages.

Chiefs were sometimes appointed by tribal councils, but often the position was inherited. A Shawnee chief was chosen because of his or her special talents as a leader, warrior, orator (public speaker), hunter, or healer.

RELIGION ▪ All things in nature, including trees, rocks, the sun, moon, stars, animals, even pumpkins and corn, were sacred to the Shawnees. Each had a spirit or soul. Dances, prayers, and chants were used to seek the spirits' help in solving daily problems and in planning the future.

A Shawnee chief named Qua-ta-wa-pea (also called Colonel Lewis), wearing the king's medal.

*In this painting, a shaman (upper left) is preparing
to enter a sweat lodge with an ailing man, while
a "witch" (lower right) is trying to use "evil magic"
to prevent the healing. The Shawnees believed that
both illness and health were the work of spirits.*

The vision quest was an important Shawnee ritual. Children ages seven and up and adults would fast, cleanse themselves in a sweat lodge, and go off alone into the woods. There they would await a vision in which their guardian spirit would appear to them to offer guidance.

To all Native Americans the Great Spirit was a force that ruled all nature. The Shawnees also worshipped a female deity they called Our Grandmother (or Pa-po-ok-we, which means "cloud"). They believed Our Grandmother created the Shawnees and taught them how to live and work. Then she returned to the sky where she lived with her grandson, Cloudy Boy, and his little dog. One day Our Grandmother would drop a huge net down to collect her chosen people, the good Shawnees, and bring them to live with her in heaven.

Evil spirits were believed to cause sickness. Disease was rare among Native Americans until they encountered European traders, explorers, and settlers. Shawnee healers called shamans treated the sick and wounded with herbs, roots, charms, and prayers. They could also set broken bones.

CEREMONIES • The Shawnees showed their appreciation for the spirits' help by holding special ceremonies. In spring and fall, tribal dances of thanksgiving were held, and in late summer, the corn harvest was celebrated.

At the spring Bread Dance, women's role as farmer and gatherer was honored and the Shawnees prayed for an abundant harvest. They feasted on roast game and cornbread, sang traditional songs, played drums, rattles, and flutes, and danced for hours.

The fall Bread Dance was similar, but this time men's role as hunter was celebrated and prayers were offered for plentiful winter game. Thanks were also given for the harvest.

In August the Green Corn Dance lasted for several days. It was also a time when the less serious crimes of the villagers were forgiven. The Shawnees also held ceremonies for naming infants and burying the dead.

Well-known Native American artist Ernest Spybuck's watercolor painting of the Shawnee's Bread Dance ceremony.

WARFARE ▪ Intertribal warfare was an important part of Shawnee life. It was a way to seek honor and glory, to show courage, particularly for young men, and to settle disputes between tribes. A tribal council was held to decide whether to go to war. The Shawnees might circulate a wampum belt or a tomahawk smeared with red clay among neighboring villages to invite them to join a war party.

Before the warriors departed (and if they returned victorious), a dance and feast were held. A shaman traveled with the war party to treat the wounded. He might carry a buckskin pack called a sacred bundle. A sacred bundle contained objects such as animal bones, feathers, and tiny carvings the Shawnees believed gave them special powers.

Warriors used stone tomahawks, war clubs, and bows and arrows. By the mid-1700s the Shawnees had acquired metal knives and hatchets, and guns and ammunition. They bound their prisoners with decorated sashes called prisoner ties and marched them back to the village.

Some prisoners were made to run the gauntlet. This was a double line of Shawnee men, women, and children holding clubs and sticks. Prisoners who made it through the gauntlet won the respect of their captors and often their lives were spared. They might be held as hostages, made slaves, or adopted by the tribe.

Later, warfare was not only between tribes. The Shawnees would find their lives and land constantly threatened by white intruders. Eventually the Indian warriors proved to be no match for the trained, professional armies of the Europeans and Americans and their sophisticated weaponry. A period of almost constant hostilities in the Eastern Woodlands began in the mid-1700s and continued for more than sixty years.

Chapter Four

LIVING OFF
THE LAND

Shawnee life revolved around the seasons. There was not enough wildlife or dried meat and vegetables to feed an entire community all year long. After each harvest, a Shawnee settlement broke into smaller groups and left for distant winter camps in sheltered valleys.

In early spring the Shawnees returned to their summer villages. These more permanent settlements sometimes remained in the same place for twenty years or more.

HOUSES AND VILLAGES ▪ The Shawnees lived in dome-shaped lodges clustered beside a river, lake, or stream. There were between twenty and three hundred dwellings in a village. Around the village might be a palisade, or protective fence of tall, sharpened sticks.

A lodge was constructed by driving saplings into the ground in a circle or oval, then lashing the tops together with

*An early Shawnee village. Each bark-covered lodge had
a frame of bent and tied saplings, as can be seen on the left.*

rawhide thongs. The frame was then covered with overlapping
animal skins or sheets of flattened bark. A hole was left in the
roof to let out smoke from the cooking fire. There were no
windows; over the door opening hung a skin or blanket.

The lodge had one large room in which a family cooked, ate,
slept, played, and prayed. There were rush mats, animal skins,
or blankets on the floor. Some Shawnees made raised platforms
of sticks and branches for their beds.

In each lodge was a kettle for washing, a supply of cooking utensils, bowls, and platters made of bark, bone, horn, pottery, or wood, and baskets for storage. Extra clothing and other belongings were hung from the roof supports.

A good-sized village usually had a *msi-kah-mi-qui* (em-SEE-kaa-MEE-kee), or council house, in its center. This dwelling, of hewn logs, was stronger and much bigger than a lodge. It could be 30 feet wide by 80 feet long or larger and was used for ceremonies, councils, and as protection during an attack.

COMMUNITY LIFE ▪ Family was important to the Shawnees. Aunts and uncles, grandparents, cousins, and in-laws lived in nearby lodges or shared one dwelling if it was large enough.

In the summer, villagers tended crops, hunted game, and gathered wild foods. Summer was also a time for socializing. Family gatherings, festivals, ceremonies, dances, and tribal councils were held. There was much visiting among villages, and women would keep the stewpot going all day.

Fertile soil, a moderate climate, and sufficient rainfall made the Eastern Woodlands ideal for farming. Each family had its own plot, but what was grown, gathered, or hunted by a community was shared.

Men and women had specific roles in Shawnee society. The women were farmers, gatherers, and craftspeople; the men were hunters, traders, and warriors.

In spring, men cleared the fields and women and children prepared the soil using hoes and digging tools made from branches and animal bones. The Shawnees grew corn, squash, pumpkins, beans, sweet potatoes, and tobacco.

Shawnee men and women had definite and separate roles to play in community life, but worked together to make the village run smoothly.

Corn was the Shawnee's most important crop. It was eaten on the cob after being roasted, steamed, or boiled. The corn might be dried and the kernels ground into cornmeal, which was used to make cornbread.

Wild rice that grew in the marshes was harvested from canoes the Shawnees made from sheets of flattened bark laced together with wild grapevines. In northern areas maple and hickory sap were gathered to make sugar and syrup. Wild po-

Shawneecake

Some people believe that johnnycake, a kind of corn bread, got its name from the word Shawneecake. Here is a simple recipe for johnnycake.

¾ cup flour
1½ cups yellow cornmeal
2 tablespoons sugar
4 teaspoons baking powder
1 teaspoon salt
2 eggs, beaten
1¼ cups milk
¼ cup salad oil

Mix dry ingredients by hand or with an electric mixer, then add liquids and beat until smooth.

Place batter in a greased 8-by-12-inch pan and bake at 400° Fahrenheit for about 30 minutes.

Best when served warm.

tatoes, onions, nuts, berries, roots, and honey were gathered in the woods. Some berries and roots were made into teas and medicines.

HUNTING ▪ Long before farming provided much of their food, the Shawnees were hunters. They used every part of an animal: the meat for food, the fur and skin for clothing and blankets, the fat for cooking, the sinew (tendon) for sewing thread, the organs for medicines and ceremonies, and the bones for tools and needles.

The men hunted squirrels, skunks, wild turkeys, rabbits, raccoons, deer, bear, elk, moose, and caribou. Hunters on ponies or on foot used bows and arrows, stone knives, slingshots, or clubs. The clubs were made from deerskin-covered rocks attached to strong sticks. Hunters imitated animal calls and disguised themselves in animal skins in order to sneak up on their prey.

The Shawnees also fished with spears and nets. They caught otters and beavers, using traps made of poles rigged with a rawhide noose. An honor system was followed; no Shawnee would ever rob another's trap.

CLOTHING ▪ Shawnee dress was simple and practical for the woodlands environment. Women sewed soft deerskins into shirts, leggings, and breechcloths for the men and into shirts and wrap skirts for themselves.

They made soft-soled moccasins that had ankle flaps and bead trim. Garments might be decorated with dyed porcupine quills, feathers, beads, and ribbons, and the skins could be colored with animal and vegetable dyes.

A roach headdress made of animal hair, with a single golden eagle tail feather set in a bone tube so that it would stand upright.

Men wore cloth headbands to which they added owl, hawk, or eagle feathers. Roach headpieces were a distinctive Shawnee accessory. These were made from deer or porcupine hair that was pushed through a bone spreader so that it stood straight up. Attached to the headpiece were one to three feathers.

Shawnee men favored jewelry. They wore copper or silver armlets, bracelets, and necklaces; chokers made of shells or bone; and bone and silver nose rings and earrings.

CRAFTS ▪ Many Shawnee garments and household items could be considered works of art. Women made mats from bark, rushes, and other fibers. Shawnee baskets were woven so closely they could hold water or loosely enough to serve as sieves or sifters.

The Shawnees fashioned wampum belts from strings of shells or glass beads woven together into heavy sashes about 5 feet long and 4 inches wide. The symbols, colors, and designs on each belt told a story, outlined terms of a treaty, or relayed a message. A blackbird symbol meant bad news, for example, and a buried hatchet or a setting sun represented peace.

A Shawnee water drum and drumstick (left), and a coconut shell rattle (right), used for social and ceremonial dances.

GAMES ▪ Shawnee life was not all work and no play. Villagers loved games of chance, ball games, and foot races. They enjoyed a form of football that they played before certain ceremonies such as the Bread Dance.

Players used a buckskin ball, smaller than a modern football, that was stuffed with deer hair. Men and boys had to kick the ball while women and girls could also carry it. It was a rough and lively game in which pushing, shoving, and intercepting passes were allowed. Wooden pegs stuck into the ground kept track of the score. The losing team gathered the firewood for the ceremony that followed.

Chapter Five

THE SHAWNEE RESISTANCE

When white people began to settle in the eastern region of North America, as many as a million Native Americans — belonging to about sixty tribes — lived there.

The Shawnees first encountered European explorers and traders in the 1500s. The Spanish came north from Florida. Later the French and then the British arrived, landing on the shores of the Atlantic Ocean and slowly moving west.

These early travelers did not want the Indians' land. They had come to search for treasures such as gold and silver. Trading between Europeans and Native Americans flourished for many years. The Shawnees exchanged animal hides (especially deerskins) and furs for jewelry, glass beads, ribbon, metal cookware, blankets, wool and other fabrics, and steel weapons and traps.

At first the Shawnees were not hostile to these newcomers. The Europeans were curious about the native peoples but

*The French and Indian War, which was fought
mainly in the Eastern Woodlands, involved
the Shawnees, who sided with the French.*

made no attempt to conquer them. Many Indians served as their guides. Some white men married into Indian tribes and adopted their culture. Only later, when the numbers of outsiders began to increase dramatically, did the Indians become alarmed and distrustful.

By the early 1700s, missionaries and settlers from England and France began to follow the explorers and traders. The French and English began to compete for trade with the Indians and then to battle each other for control of the New World. The

Shawnees tried to stay out of the struggle but were eventually drawn in, believing that whatever side they supported would allow them to keep their homeland. Decades of bloody conflict followed, and life for the Shawnees would never be the same.

During the French and Indian War, which began in 1754, the French and the British made the Eastern Woodlands their battleground. The Shawnees sided with the French. The British, however, benefited from reinforcements and supplies sent to the colonies. They defeated the French, who then lost control of the area.

In 1763, the Treaty of Paris gave England all of North America east of the Mississippi River. But the matter of the Indians' land was not addressed. Now the Shawnees and other eastern tribes had to defend themselves from the English colonists and from other tribes, especially the powerful Iroquois, who had supported the British during the war.

The first major confrontation with the colonists took place in Shawnee territory in 1774. Daniel Boone, the American explorer and frontiersman, had scouted the area that is now Kentucky and West Virginia, and settlers began pouring in. When the Shawnees attacked the new settlements, troops were sent to burn Indian villages and send the message that they were to leave the colonists alone.

THE AMERICAN REVOLUTION ▪ In 1775, the Shawnees became involved in the war for independence fought between the thirteen American colonies and Britain. The Indians believed that a victorious British army would help them stop the flow of white settlers into Indian territory.

But the British lost the war, and in 1783 England gave the United States most of the eastern region of the country, from the Atlantic Ocean to the Mississippi River, and from the Great Lakes to Florida. Again, the Indians' rights to their land were ignored.

Now the frontier moved deeper into Indian territory. Many Shawnees moved out of the area. Others continued to resist white settlement and defend their land. They tried to make the Ohio River the boundary between United States and Indian territory and attacked any white people who attempted to cross it.

But thousands of settlers loaded their wagons and boats with food, supplies, and fencing, and drove their livestock to the new land. They brought sickness, too, against which the Native Americans had no immunity (natural resistance).

When the Indians attacked the settlers' wagons, boats, and settlements, the settlers demanded protection. Soldiers were sent into Shawnee territory.

In the late 1700s, the Shawnees fought a number of major battles. In the fall of 1791, the Shawnee chief Blue Jacket, a white man who had been adopted by the tribe as a teenager, helped organize 3,000 warriors to make a surprise attack on U.S. army troops along the Wabash River in Indiana.

During the battle, 630 Americans were killed and some 300 more were wounded — compared to 21 Indians killed and 40 wounded. It was the most one-sided defeat in history of a United States army by Native American forces.

The Shawnees were not always victorious. In August 1794, a combined Indian force of 2,000 warriors was overwhelmed by

At the Battle of Fallen Timbers in 1794, the Shawnee forces, led by Chief Blue Jacket (at right in the painting above), were badly outnumbered.

U.S. General "Mad Anthony" Wayne's forces at the Battle of Fallen Timbers, fought near present-day Toledo, Ohio. Afterward, Wayne and his men roamed up and down the Maumee River, burning Shawnee villages and destroying their crops.

Almost a year after the battle, Wayne convened a council at Fort Greenville, on the Indiana and Ohio border. He wanted to purchase a large portion of Indian land. More than 1,000 warriors and chiefs representing twelve tribes attended. The council lasted two months.

Finally the chiefs, including Blue Jacket, felt they had no choice but to sign a treaty. Most of Ohio, a large part of Indiana, and the places called Chicago and Detroit, an area totaling 25,000 square miles, were ceded, or sold, to the United States.

The Shawnees were to be given $20,000 worth of goods immediately and $9,000 in goods and supplies each year after that. The land — home to the Shawnees — had been sold for less than a penny an acre. The Old Northwest was officially opened to white settlement.

One Shawnee who refused to attend the council was enraged at its outcome. He said this to Blue Jacket: "My heart is a stone: heavy with sadness for my people; cold with the knowledge that no treaty will keep the whites out of our lands; hard with the determination to resist as long as I live and breathe." That Shawnee was the famous warrior Tecumseh.

"Sheltowee"

DANIEL BOONE AND THE SHAWNEES

Few people knew that Daniel Boone, the famous explorer and frontiersman, once lived among the Indians as a Shawnee brave.

While hunting in the Ohio Valley in January 1778, Boone and twenty-six of his men were captured by a large party of Shawnee and Delaware Indians. Boone, who could speak some Shawnee, agreed to surrender if the Indians would not hurt his men.

Boone was made to run the gauntlet, and his courage during this ordeal impressed his captors.

Black Fish, a Shawnee chief who was also the adoptive father of ten-year-old Tecumseh, took the forty-four-year-old frontiersman as his son. Boone was given the name "Sheltowee," which means Big Turtle.

Boone adapted easily to Shawnee life. He wore body paint and deerskin garments. He learned to speak the language fluently, excelled at tribal games and foot races, and was a skilled hunter.

But secretly Boone was thinking only of escape. He had gone along with the adoption so that he could learn about the Shawnees' plan to attack white settlements in Kentucky.

One day in June, five months after his capture, he had a chance to flee. Boone leaped onto his horse and galloped into the woods. He rode until his horse collapsed, then began running until he reached the Ohio River. There he built a crude raft on which he floated his clothing, rifle, and ammunition, and swam behind it across the river. By the time he reached Fort Boonesboro, near present-day Lexington, Kentucky, he had covered 160 miles in four days.

Months later Boone found himself defending the fort against his "father," Black Fish, and the Shawnee warriors. After nine days of fierce fighting, the Shawnees retreated. The Battle of Boonesboro helped the United States win control of Kentucky and is considered an important conflict of the Revolutionary War.

Daniel Boone continued to hunt and explore the frontier for many years. He died in Missouri in 1820, at the age of eighty-six.

Chapter Six

THE WARRIOR
AND THE PROPHET

Tecumseh and a small group of followers lived and hunted in southern Ohio, even though it was now United States land. Although white settlers were everywhere, Tecumseh refused to recognize the treaty and vowed that no more Indian land would be lost, even though U.S. officials used bribes, trickery, alcohol, and threats to get tribal chiefs to sign away their land.

IN SEARCH OF A LEADER ▪ Many of the Shawnees who had not yet left the Ohio Valley settled near U.S. military posts and became dependent on government food and supplies. They were bewildered and spiritless. The Indians in the Old Northwest looked to Tecumseh, who was now chief of the remaining Shawnees, for leadership.

Tecumseh still believed it was possible to stop the takeover of Indian land. "Now we are weak and many of our people are afraid," he told his followers. "But someday I will embrace our brother tribes and draw them into a bundle, and together we will win our country back from the whites."

He found support where he least expected it. Tecumseh had a brother named Lalawethika (la-la-we-THEE-kuh), meaning "the rattle," because he had been a noisy child.

Unlike his siblings, Lalawethika grew up to be a bully and a troublemaker, a poor hunter, and a reluctant warrior. He drank heavily and was unpopular with members of his tribe. Blinded in his right eye by a childhood hunting accident, he had a gruesome appearance. But at age thirty-four, Lalawethika had undergone a remarkable transformation. He had fallen into a deep trance for many hours and later said the Great Spirit had given him a message that he was to carry to all his people and to the other eastern tribes.

The Indians were to abandon white ways, refuse white goods (including alcohol), and return to the old ways of their people. If they obeyed, the Great Spirit would make the white people disappear, restore the Shawnees' land, and return their dead relatives to life.

Lalawethika changed his name to Tenskwatawa (TENS-kwa-TAH-wuh), which means "the open door," and proclaimed himself the Shawnee Prophet. He traveled to villages far and wide to spread his message.

Tecumseh the warrior and Tenskwatawa the prophet were a powerful team. They began to fire up an Indian resistance movement, much to the alarm of Major General William Henry Harrison, who was governor of the Indiana Territory.

The brothers established a Shawnee village in 1808 on a site near the junction of the Wabash and Tippecanoe rivers.

Tecumseh's brother, Tenskwatawa the Prophet, in a painting by George Catlin.

This was clearly a defiant gesture, for the land had been sold by other Indian chiefs to the government. The settlement, with some 1,000 Indians from tribes all over the East, was named Prophet's Town, but it was also called Tippecanoe Village.

In 1809, Tecumseh set out on the most important journey of his life. He began traveling from the Great Lakes to Florida, visiting every tribe in the region and pleading with them to stop selling their land and to join together into a great alliance.

While Tecumseh was away Harrison pressured a group of chiefs to sell 3 million acres of land in Indiana country. When the Shawnee leader returned many months later he was enraged and vowed to take action.

THE BATTLE OF TIPPECANOE ▪ In August 1811, Tecumseh led hundreds of Indians in war canoes down the Wabash River to meet with Harrison at his Vincennes estate. Through his interpreter, Tecumseh told Harrison he was angry about the treaties and that they should be canceled. "No tribe has the right to sell, even to each other, much less to strangers," he declared. "Sell a country? Why not sell the air, the clouds, and the great sea as well as the earth?" Harrison argued that the treaties were valid and that individual chiefs had the right to sell Indian land.

This lithograph shows the confrontation between Tecumseh and Major General William Henry Harrison at Harrison's estate in 1811. Tecumseh was furious over the sale of Indian lands.

At the Battle of Tippecanoe, Harrison (at left in the lithograph) and his troops forced the Shawnees to retreat.

Harrison knew Tecumseh presented a real threat. He immediately requested reinforcements, and an entire regiment was sent to the frontier. Tecumseh resumed his quest to unite the eastern tribes. "Will we let ourselves be destroyed without a struggle?" he asked the Creeks in Alabama. "I know you will cry with me, 'Never! Never!' "

Harrison knew he had to stop the Shawnees. He decided to attack Prophet's Town while Tecumseh was away. Harrison marched his army of 1,000 soldiers north along the Wabash River, but Tenskwatawa's scouts learned of his approach.

Before dawn on a frosty November day, Tenskwatawa's warriors launched the Battle of Tippecanoe by attacking Harrison's camp. The Shawnee Prophet, who had assured his followers they would be protected by his powerful medicine, positioned himself a safe distance from the fighting. Although the Indians outnumbered the Americans, Harrison and his soldiers stood their ground. Bullets flew and warriors began to fall.

When they saw that his magic was not working, Tenskwatawa's followers began to retreat. Harrison then led his troops into Prophet's Town and burned it to the ground.

Tecumseh returned home, consumed with rage and sorrow. "You have destroyed everything I have tried to accomplish," he said to his brother, who was being held captive by some of his former followers. "You are no Shawnee — no prophet. Go!" And with that Tenskwatawa was exiled from the tribe. He spent the rest of his life as a drifter.

WAR OF 1812 ▪ The following spring, America was again at war with Britain. English ships had been attacking American vessels. The War of 1812 broke out in Canada. The Shawnees agreed to join the British because Tecumseh believed it was the tribe's last chance to save their land.

He organized a force of 2,000 warriors from several tribes and was made its commander. Major General Isaac Brock commissioned Tecumseh a brigadier general in the British army, an extraordinary gesture, and gave him an officer's sword, pistols, and red dress coat. Their combined army managed to drive the Americans out of the Great Lakes area and to capture Fort Detroit, forcing U.S. General William Hull and 2,200 soldiers to surrender. It would be their last victory.

Brock was killed in a distant battle and was replaced by Brigadier General Henry A. Procter, who treated the Indians poorly and was not a strong leader. The British began to lose control of the upper Great Lakes area. A turning point came with a U.S. naval victory on Lake Erie, when Lieutenant Oliver Hazard Perry captured an entire English fleet.

Procter wanted to retreat beyond the Canadian border. When he realized the British were breaking their promise to help the Indians, Tecumseh began to lose heart. Hundreds of his warriors went home, but Tecumseh resolved he would fight until the end.

Tecumseh convinced Procter to make a stand against Harrison's troops on the Thames River. But the battle ended in an American victory and cost Tecumseh his life. No one knows if he could have created an Indian confederacy had he lived. He might have eventually realized that uniting so many scattered tribes, some of whom had been traditional enemies, would be an impossible task.

The war ended in 1815, but none of the issues that prompted the conflict were settled. Harrison, however, was seen as a hero. He would be elected the ninth president of the United States in 1840, using as his campaign slogan "Tippecanoe and Tyler, Too," a reference to his victory at Prophet's Town and to his running mate, John Tyler.

Tecumseh became a legendary figure to generations of Native Americans. His spirit and determination inspired the western tribes, who continued the struggle to defend their lands until the end of the century.

After Tecumseh's death the remaining Shawnees in the Old Northwest were without a leader. The last of the tribe began to depart, at first willingly and later by force. Some Shawnees joined groups of their people who had gone earlier to Missouri and Illinois. Others went to Kansas and Texas.

William Henry Harrison used the victory at Tippecanoe in his successful campaign for the presidency in 1840.

REMOVAL ▪ In 1830, Congress passed the Indian Removal Act, which moved the remaining eastern tribes beyond the Mississippi River.

Groups of Native Americans, including the Ohio Valley and Great Lakes tribes, were uprooted from their ancestral homes and sent west to newly established Indian Territory (present-day Oklahoma). Some 60,000 people made the long, difficult journey. Thousands died along the way from cold, hunger, sickness, and sorrow.

Those who survived found their new environment strange and unwelcoming. Working the dry land was difficult, and there was not enough game to hunt. The government offered little help in the form of training or tools to farm the new land.

Like other relocated Native Americans, the Shawnees were forced to abandon their culture and traditions and to adopt white ways. Their children were sent away to boarding schools and forbidden to speak their native languages or wear native dress.

At first the Shawnees were contained on Oklahoma reservations, parcels of land the government set aside for Indians. But in 1887, Congress passed the Dawes Act, which led to the elimination of the reservations. Small parcels of reservation land were assigned to individual Native Americans. The rest was opened to white settlement.

During the late 1880s, thousands of settlers swarmed into Oklahoma, competing for land in what came to be known as the Oklahoma Land Rush. Just before noon on April 22, 1889, nearly 50,000 people gathered in central Oklahoma, waiting for the sound of a pistol shot that would signal the opening of Indian lands. They then raced on horseback, on foot, or in wagons to make their claims.

Despite being made United States citizens in 1901, the Shawnees in Oklahoma endured many hardships. They tried to make a living by farming and ranching, but when deposits of valuable natural resources, including gas and petroleum, were discovered on some of their land in the early 1900s, their homes were again threatened.

Some were able to resist, but others sold their property, often for less than it was worth, and ended up in poverty. Finally the government began to address the problems of displaced Native Americans. Congress passed the Oklahoma Indian Welfare Act in 1936.

In a race across the plains to stake land claims,
thousands of settlers participated in the
Oklahoma Land Rush on April 22, 1889.

Under this law Native Americans could organize into groups and seek a charter from the government. These newly formed bands could qualify for financial aid and other government benefits. The law also canceled an earlier government order that prohibited the practice of tribal customs and the speaking of native languages.

Since then, other laws have been passed to protect the rights of the Shawnees and other Native Americans and to make it possible for them to obtain government assistance, including vocational training and education, to give them a voice in the federal government, and to help them protect their heritage.

A painting by Ernest Spybuck shows a Shawnee homestead around the turn of the century.

Chapter Seven

THE SHAWNEES TODAY

Although people of Shawnee descent are scattered throughout the United States, most live in either Oklahoma or Ohio. Many actively practice Shawnee traditions and rituals.

THE OKLAHOMA SHAWNEES ▪ There are three major Shawnee groups in Oklahoma: the Absentee Shawnee Tribe, the Eastern Shawnee Tribe, and the Loyal (or Cherokee) Shawnee Tribe.

Approximately 12,500 Shawnees are formally enrolled in these tribes, but not all of them live close to tribal headquarters or participate in tribal life. They live not on reservations but on privately owned land. Many Shawnees have achieved success in various fields — as ranchers, farmers, tradespeople, artists, or in other professions.

The Shawnees have their own tribal governments made up of elected officials. These officials work to obtain sources of funding for their members and to serve as a liaison (connection) between the tribe and the state and federal governments.

The Shawnees, like other Native American groups, celebrate their heritage by performing traditional ceremonies and dances.

Some Shawnee Words

Shawnee is one of the many Algonquian languages. It can still be heard on ceremonial occasions and is spoken by a small number of tribal elders.

Here are some Shawnee words. They were provided by the Eastern Shawnee tribe, which has compiled a dictionary of Shawnee words for public schools in the region.

nekkaen (nek-CAIN)	mother
nechenenah (nek-ke-NEE-nah)	brother
p'so (PEE-SO)	howdy (hello)
niw-ya-wa (nee-YAH-wah)	I thank you
ah' (ah)	yes
ma'hatah (MAH-tah)	no
taquana (tah-KWAH-nah)	bread
wa'pee (wah-PEE)	cold
k'sta (ki-STA)	hot
konah (KO-nah)	snow

THE OHIO SHAWNEES ▪ After Tecumseh's death in 1813, those Shawnees who remained in the Ohio Valley lived quietly. Their descendants make up the 600 members of the Shawnee Nation United Remnant Band (URB) in Ohio. The URB was officially recognized by the state in 1980 and began purchasing tribal lands in 1989. One 117-acre landholding in Shawandasse in west central Ohio serves as a gathering place for ceremonies, councils, and youth camps.

LEGACY ▪ Although the four groups of Shawnees are separate entities, they have begun working together to preserve their history and culture. They are exploring the possibility of creating a Shawnee museum.

There are many reminders today of the Shawnees and their leader, Tecumseh. Towns called Shawnee can be found in Oklahoma, Kansas, Colorado, Ohio, and Wyoming (Tennessee's town is called Sewanee). The Suwannee (Swanee) River, which runs through Florida and Georgia, was named for the tribe. Tecumseh's name was given to towns in Oklahoma, Nebraska, Michigan, and Ontario, Canada. Many children were named after the Shawnee chief—even white infants. Ohio-born William Tecumseh Sherman, an American Civil War general, was one.

In recent years there has been a reawakened national interest in Native American culture. Like many other tribes, the Shawnees are intent on preserving their heritage. They honor the memory of Tecumseh and his dream of Indian unity. "A single twig breaks easily," Tecumseh once said of his people, "but the bundle of twigs is strong."

A SHAWNEE LEGEND:
THE PANTHER CROUCHING

The story of Tecumseh's birth has become a Shawnee legend. It begins on a clear, cold late-winter night in the Ohio wilderness. A Shawnee woman was resting on a blanket of cedar boughs and deerskins in a special lodge reserved for women giving birth. Suddenly there was a brilliant flash of greenish white that lit up the sky. It was a meteor, streaking across the heavens.

At the same moment, the cry of an infant shattered the stillness. The village elders were amazed. The meteor was a good omen, they said. A shooting star in the Shawnee religion represented a panther, a powerful being in the spirit world.

The infant was named Tecumseh, which means "the panther crouching." He was born sometime in the early spring of 1768, in his family's village of Piqua Town, near present-day Springfield, Ohio. As a boy, Tecumseh excelled at games, sports, and hunting, and he was a natural leader.

Tecumseh realized early in life that he could move others with his words. While still a teenager he was able to convince a group of Shawnee warriors to stop the practice of torturing prisoners.

Tecumseh envisioned a great alliance of all the tribes east of the Mississippi River. It would be powerful enough to stop the Americans from taking any more of their land. His efforts won him the respect even of his enemies. This famous Shawnee is remembered as a great orator (public speaker) and diplomat, and a fierce fighter in the struggle to defend his native land.

IMPORTANT DATES

1530s	Shawnees encounter Spanish explorers in the Eastern Woodlands of North America
1650s	French and English explorers and traders arrive in Shawnee territory
1754–1763	Shawnees side with the French against the British during the French and Indian War
1768	Tecumseh is born in the Ohio wilderness
1775–1783	Shawnees fight with the British against the colonists in the American Revolution
1790–1794	Shawnee warriors battle U.S. army in Indian territory
1795	Greenville Treaty signed; Old Northwest is opened to white settlement
1808	Prophet's Town (Tippecanoe Village) is established on the Wabash River in Indiana country

1811	Major General William Henry Harrison's forces destroy Prophet's Town in the Battle of Tippecanoe
1812	In the War of 1812, the Shawnees fight with the British against the United States
1813	Tecumseh is killed in the Battle of Thames
1830	Congress passes the Indian Removal Act
1887	Dawes Act opens reservation land to white settlement
1936	Oklahoma Indian Welfare Act allows Native Americans to form groups and receive government funds and services
1980	The Shawnee Nation United Remnant Band (URB) is officially recognized by the state of Ohio and begins buying back tribal lands in central Ohio

GLOSSARY

alliance. Individuals or groups united for a common goal.

charter. A written contract provided by an authority to establish a group and define its powers.

deity. A person, animal, or object believed to have special powers; a god or goddess.

migrate. To leave one country, region, or place in order to settle in another.

Msi-kah-mi-qui. A Shawnee council house.

Pa-po-ok-we. "Our Grandmother," the female Shawnee deity.

prophet. One believed to have the ability to foresee the future and to reveal to his or her followers the will of a higher power.

quest. A search for knowledge or insight; an adventurous journey.

ritual. A ceremony established by tradition.

treaty. An agreement or settlement reached after a formal meeting.

wampum. Beads made of polished shells strung together in strands and used by Native Americans as money or ornaments.

AUTHOR'S NOTE

The author wishes to thank Don Greenfeather, chairman of the Loyal Shawnee Tribe; George J. Captain, chief of the Eastern Shawnee Tribe, and his son, Nelis Captain, tribal planner; and Anthony Plaza, records management coordinator for the Absentee Shawnee Tribe.

Also helpful in the writing of this book were sources found in the Huntington Free Library in the Bronx, New York, which serves as the library for the National Museum of the American Indian.

The dialogue included in this book appears in several sources used by the author, and either includes actual conversations taken from historical records or what is generally believed to have been said.

BIBLIOGRAPHY

*Books for children

Billard, Jules B., ed. *The World of the American Indian.* Washington, D.C.: National Geographic Society, 1993.

Calloway, Colin G. *Indians of the Northeast.* New York: Facts On File, 1991.

*Cavan, Seamus. *Daniel Boone and the Opening of the Ohio Country.* New York: Chelsea House Publishers, 1991.

*Dockstader, Frederick J. *Great North American Indians.* New York: Van Nostrand Reinhold Co., 1977.

Eckert, Allan W. *Gateway to Empire.* Boston: Little, Brown & Co., 1983.

Eckert, Allan W. *A Sorrow in Our Heart.* New York: Bantam Books, 1992.

Force, Roland W. and Maryanne Tefft Force. *The American Indians.* New York: Chelsea House Publishers, 1991.

*Fulkerson, Chuck. *The Shawnee*. Vero Beach, Fla.: Rourke Publications, Inc., 1992.

*Georgakas, Dan. *The Broken Hoop*. Garden City, N.Y.: Doubleday and Co., Inc., 1973.

Gilbert, Bil. *God Gave Us This Country*. New York: Atheneum Press, 1989.

Gridley, Marion E. *Contemporary American Indian Leaders*. New York: Dodd, Mead & Company, 1972.

Hook, Jason. *American Indian Warrior Chiefs*. Poole, Dorset (England): Firebird Books, 1990.

Icenhower, Joseph B. *Tecumseh and the Indian Confederation 1811–1813*. New York: Franklin Watts, Inc., 1975.

*Kent, Zachary. *Tecumseh*. Chicago: Childrens Press, 1992.

Liptak, Karen. *North American Indian Tribal Chiefs*. New York: Franklin Watts, Inc., 1992.

Shorto, Russell. *Tecumseh (And the Dream of an American Indian Nation)*. Englewood Cliffs, N.J.: Silver Burdett Press, 1989.

Trigger, Bruce G., ed. *Handbook of North American Indians*. Washington, D.C.: Smithsonian Institution, 1978.

Utley, Robert M. and Welcome E. Washburn. *Indian Wars*. Boston: Houghton Mifflin Co., 1977.

Viola, Herman J. *After Columbus. The Smithsonian Chronicle of the North American Indian*. Washington, D.C.: Smithsonian Books, 1990.

INDEX

Page numbers in *italics* refer to illustrations.